TASTE THE WORLD!
CHOCOLATE
AF230979
WORLD BOOK
www.worldbook.com

Table of Contents

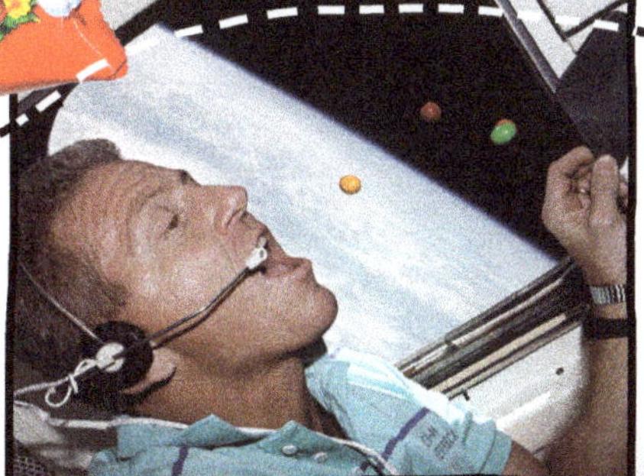

BEFORE YOU BEGIN

Included in this book are a few recipes that allow you to "taste the world!" Before you begin, look on page 46 for some helpful hints. Read the recipes carefully and always ask an adult to help—especially when handling knives or using the stove. Besides, cooking is easier and more fun when you work together!

As we travel around the world, we'll explore my history, discover some fun facts, and learn to prepare some delicious recipes. Along the way, you may read words that are new to you. If I can explain what a word means easily, I'll do it right where you are reading. If I use the word many times, or if the explanation is complicated, I will put the word in **boldface** (type that **looks like this**). Boldface words are defined in a glossary in the back of the book.

CHOCOLATE?

Chocolate is made from cacao. Cacao is a seed, or bean, found inside the fruit pods that grow on the trunk of the tropical cacao tree. It is **indigenous** (native) to Central and South America. Cacao trees are also grown in the Caribbean, southeastern Asia, and West Africa.

Cacao beans must go through several stages in order to develop the chocolate flavor. First, the fruit pod is cracked open and the beans, which are covered in a sweet white pulp, are scooped out. The beans are placed in boxes and allowed to **ferment** for several days. While the beans are fermenting, the pulp turns into liquid and drains off.

Next, the beans are dried in the sun and packed in bags for shipment. Manufacturers roast the beans, remove the shells, and grind the beans into a thick paste. When the paste dries, it turns into a solid. At this point, the cacao is flavorful, but very bitter.

A WHOLE LOT OF BEANS

It takes 400 cacao beans to make one pound of chocolate. Each cacao pod holds 20 to 40 beans.

DID YOU KNOW that cacao beans with the shells removed are called **nibs?** The nibs will become chocolate.

LATIN AMERICA

In the beginning, people did not eat chocolate, they drank it! The drink was made from a ground paste of cacao beans mixed with water.

The Mayo-Chinchipe people, who lived in what is now Ecuador, may have been the first people to cultivate cacao, around 3500 B.C. By about 1200 B.C., the ancient Olmec were cultivating cacao in southern Mexico and drinking cacao beverages in religious ceremonies.

The Maya and Aztec of Central America and Mexico also learned of the delicious taste of chocolate. The Maya were trading with cacao beans as early as 600 B.C. By A.D. 1500, the Aztec were sweetening their cacao water with honey and adding ground chili powder and vanilla.

IT'S MAGIC!

Both the Maya and the Aztec considered the cacao bean to have magical powers and bring wisdom to those who drank it. They also believed it helped to cure certain illnesses and could be used as a cure for poison.

The Maya believed that chocolate was a gift from the gods. They drank it only for feasts and special ceremonies, such as births, marriages, and deaths. All Maya could drink this special treat. The Aztec, however, thought this drink was too special for everyone to drink. Only those with power and wealth could drink it.

DID YOU KNOW that the Maya drank their chocolate warm, while the Aztec preferred to drink it cold? Warm or cold, it was a special drink that was served in tall decorated containers.

CASHIN' IN ON THE CACAO BEAN

The cacao bean was considered so valuable that the Maya used it as money while trading with the Aztec. Everyday items, such as corn and other foods, clothing, taxes, and even slaves, could be traded for cacao beans.

THE PRICE OF BEANS!

Goods were sold by the bean. For example, a pumpkin would cost 4 beans; a rabbit would cost 8 or 10 beans; and a slave would cost 100 beans. Having a pocketful of cacao beans was like having a pocketful of gold today!

Almost every Maya could enjoy cacao because they lived in the right place, the hot and humid rain forests of Central America where cacao grows. The Aztec, on the other hand, could not grow cacao in the dry climate of central Mexico. So the Aztec traded with the Maya for the cacao beans. Because the beans were harder for the Aztec to obtain, they became extremely valuable to them.

DID YOU KNOW the Aztec Emperor Montezuma is said to have drunk 50 goblets of chocolate drink a day? The goblets were made of pure gold. Because the emperor considered the drink more valuable than the golden goblet, he would just throw the goblet away!

FROTHY FOAM!

The most delicious part of the chocolate drink for both the Maya and the Aztec was the frothy foam on top. The air bubbles made the drink taste so much more delicious. The Aztec and the Maya made this foam by pouring the chocolate liquid from one bowl to another until it became foamy. The more distance between bowls, the more air bubbles. The Maya called it the "food of the gods."

MOLINILLO

To create the foam, the Aztec used a long-handled, wood whisk rolled back and forth between the palms of the hands. A similar instrument is used today. It is called a **molinillo.**

Traditional Mexican hot chocolate is foamy and made with such different spices as cinnamon, chili powder, and vanilla extract. Mexican chocolate has a very distinct and rich flavor. It is often found in solid form, shaped like a disk.

TRY THIS!

MEXICAN HOT CHOCOLATE
Serves 4

INGREDIENTS

½ cup water
1 tablet (approx. 3 oz.) Mexican chocolate, coarsely chopped
1 quart whole milk

½ tsp. vanilla extract
1 pinch chili powder
ground cinnamon
whipped cream

STEPS

1. In a medium saucepan, bring the water to a boil. Remove from heat and immediately add the chocolate. Stir until melted.
2. Add the milk. Return the saucepan to the stove and turn to medium heat. When mixture is hot, remove from stove. Whisk continuously until completely blended. Add vanilla extract and a pinch of chili powder. Stir well, test, and adjust to taste. If you don't have a molinillo, use a whisk to give the chocolate a frothy foam.
3. Pour into mugs and top with whipped cream and a dusting of cinnamon.

Note: Mexican chocolate tablets are available in the ethnic foods section of some grocery stores and from online merchants. If you cannot find them, you may substitute 8 ounces of semisweet chocolate chips and ¼ teaspoon of ground cinnamon.

SPAIN

The Spanish explorer Hernán Cortés brought cacao beans and the recipe for the chocolate drink to Spain following his conquest of Mexico in 1521. It was the Aztec who introduced the chocolate drink to Cortés. But it was Spanish monks who altered the recipe by turning the bitter chocolate drink into a sweet sensation. They added sugar or honey, cinnamon, and nutmeg. They left out the chili pepper and served the drink hot. The sweet additions along with the temperature change made the drink very popular with the Spanish **nobility** (upper class).

At first, the nobility only drank chocolate for energy and health or during religious ceremonies. Since cacao beans were hard to come by, the Spanish jealously guarded their chocolate drink recipe. They kept it secret from other Europeans for nearly a century.

STRANGE BEANS

It is believed that Christopher Columbus, on his explorations for Spain, found chocolate before Cortés did. Columbus seized a load of strange brown beans but passed them up because he thought they were almonds.

IT'S A FACT!
Churros con chocolate is a national breakfast favorite in Spain. Churros are crispy strips of deep-fried dough sprinkled with sugar or cinnamon and dipped in hot, thick chocolate.

BITTER WATER

The word *chocolate* may have come from *chocolatl,* a word the Spanish conquerors may have created by combining the Mayan word *xocolatl,* which means *bitter,* with the Aztec word *atl,* which means *water.*

DID YOU KNOW that the personal bodyguards of Spanish monarchs earned the nickname "los chocolateros" because they ate so much chocolate?

FRANCE

According to one account, chocolate arrived in France in 1615 when Anne of Austria, the daughter of the king of Spain, brought chocolate with her as a wedding gift for her future husband, King Louis XIII. Since chocolate was considered very valuable, it was truly a gift fit for a king!

CHOCOLATE FOR A QUEEN

At the palace of Versailles, chocolate was a favored drink. When Austrian princess Marie Antoinette married France's King Louis XVI in 1770, she brought along her personal chocolate-maker. He was given the title "Chocolate Maker to the Queen" and created special chocolate recipes just for her. The queen started each day with a steamy cup of hot chocolate.

Profiteroles are a French version of cream puffs. These tasty treats are listed on the menu in most French restaurants. The pastry balls are made with a special dough and baked until they puff up. The balls are then filled with ice cream and drizzled with warm chocolate sauce. Yum Yum!

CHOCOLATE FOR EVERYONE IN

ENGLAND

When chocolate arrived in England in the 1650's, it was a drink for the nobility and the well to do. However, if you could afford it, you could drink it no matter what your social class was.

Chocolate houses sprung up and became fashionable meeting places in England. The atmosphere inside was often rowdy. The first business that sold chocolate in London was opened in 1657 by a Frenchman.

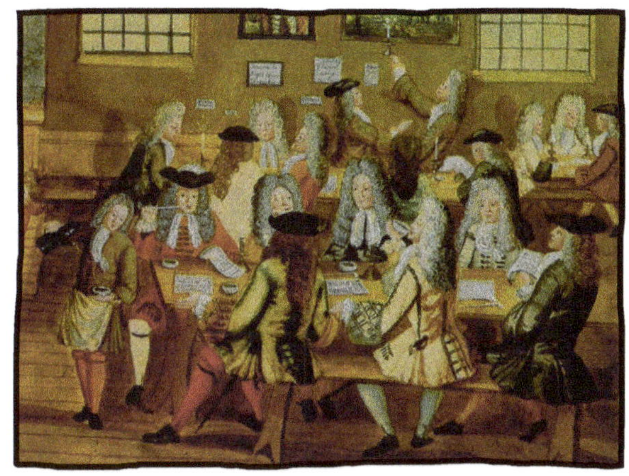

ROOM FOR CHOCOLATE

King William III had a room built at Hampton Court Palace that was used only to make chocolate.

DID YOU KNOW that chocolate has a special place in the hearts of England's royal family? Birthdays are celebrated with a special double-chocolate cake. The recipe for the family birthday cake goes all the way back to Queen Victoria. She ruled the United Kingdom from 1837 to 1901. The cake is served for the birthdays of every member of the royal family, including Queen Elizabeth II.

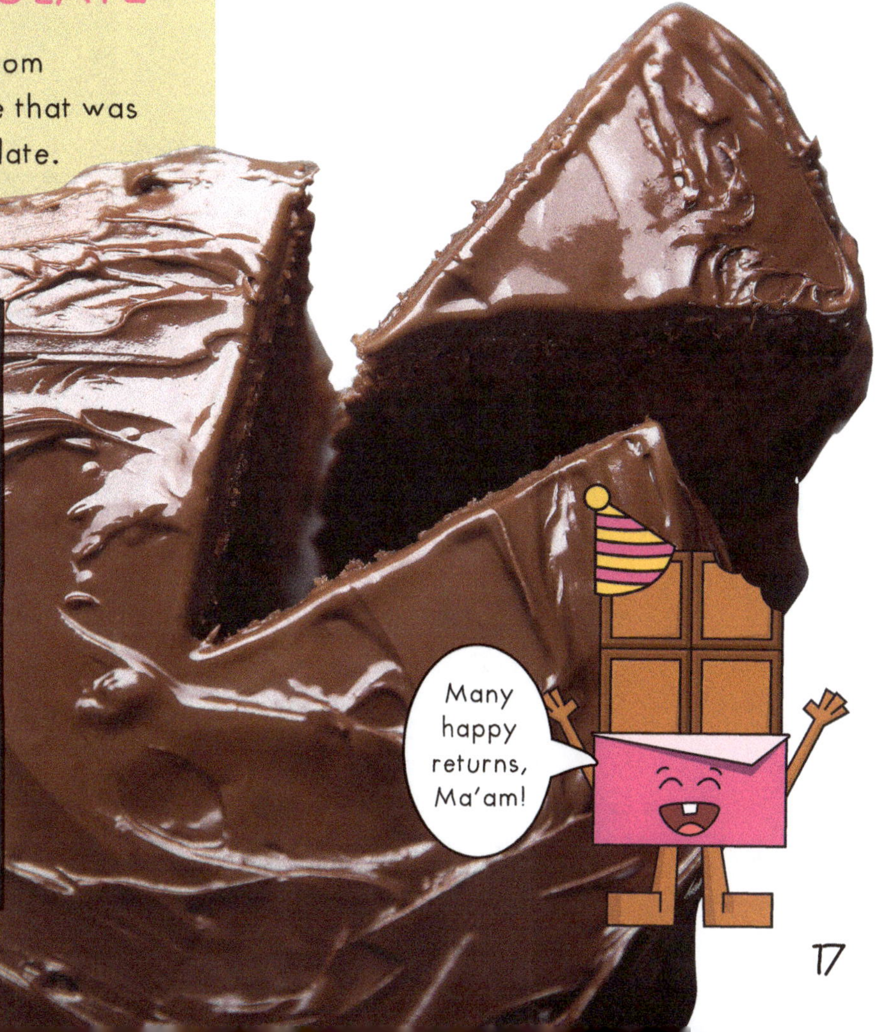

A SWEET JOB!

In the 1600's, preparing chocolate for royalty was the job to have. Imagine crafting chocolate into a wonderful treat! Today, a person who creates recipes and decorative desserts made from chocolate is called a **chocolatier.** This should not be confused with a chocolate maker, whose job is to process and manufacture chocolate.

A chocolatier uses science and art to turn mouth-watering flavors into eye-catching shapes. Chocolatiers can work in restaurants, hotels, large chocolate companies, or open their own store.

DID YOU KNOW that chocolate is a crystal and that tempering (heating and cooling it) improves the texture and appearance of chocolate? Tempered chocolate is shiny and firm, and turns smooth when it melts. If it's not tempered, it will look flat and dull.

CELEBRATE CHOCOLATE!

It's no wonder that Paris, France, is host to the original Salon du Chocolat! Master chocolatiers and chocolate lovers from around the world gather at the annual festival for a taste of chocolate heaven. The five-day festival is the world's largest event dedicated to chocolate. The chocolate sculptures are a must see!

From towering chocolate creations to small bite-size pieces, a chocolatier needs knowledge, skill, and creativity.

UNITED STATES

Chocolate first arrived in **colonial** America in 1641. A Spanish ship brought crates of chocolate to St. Augustine, Florida.

In the late 1700's the demand for chocolate grew so much that over 320 tons of cocoa beans were imported to the colonies.

The first chocolate factory in North America was set up in Dorchester, Massachusetts, in 1765 by American James Baker and Irish chocolate-maker John Hanan. They eventually began making the famous Baker's chocolate, a brand of unsweetened dark chocolate used for baking.

A REMEDY FOR RECOVERY

Some doctors in colonial America used chocolate as part of a treatment to help patients recover from smallpox, one of the most feared diseases in history. The nutrients in chocolate gave recovering patients extra energy to help them gain their weight back and build up their strength.

In the mid-1800's, new inventions made it possible to eat chocolate for the first time, rather than just drinking it. Today, such American companies as Hershey, Nestlé, and Mars sell billions of pounds of chocolate a year worldwide. It was Nestlé chocolate that led to the accidental creation of the popular American classic, chocolate chip cookies.

TRY THIS!

CHOCOLATE CHIP COOKIES

Makes 5 dozen cookies

INGREDIENTS

2 ¼ cups all-purpose flour
1 tsp. salt
1 cup (2 sticks) butter
¾ cup (150 grams) brown sugar
¾ cup (150 grams) white sugar
2 eggs, beaten

1 tsp. baking soda
1 tsp. hot water
1 tsp. vanilla
3 cups (18 oz.) semisweet chocolate chips

STEPS

1. Mix flour and salt together and set aside.
2. Melt butter and mix together with sugars. Add the eggs, mixing until combined.
3. Dissolve baking soda in hot water and add with flour mixture and butter and egg mixture.
4. Add vanilla and mix until thoroughly combined. Stir in chocolate chips. Cover and refrigerate for 36 to 48 hours.
5. Preheat oven to 375 °F (190 °C). Scoop out rounded tablespoonfuls of refrigerated dough and roll between hands into a ball. Place onto a baking sheet lined with parchment paper and press ball down to flatten. Bake for 7 to 9 minutes or until golden brown. Cool cookies on the pan for 2 minutes, then transfer to wire rack to cool completely.

WHO'S COUNTING

More than 7 billion chocolate chip cookies are eaten a year. The world's biggest chocolate chip cookie weighed over 40,000 pounds!

KINDS OF CHOCOLATE

Not all chocolate is the same, nor should it be used for the same purpose. Some chocolate is only good for cooking and baking, and some chocolate is good for eating as well as cooking.

When cacao nibs are crushed, the thick paste that is produced is called cocoa liquor. The paste contains both cocoa solids and cocoa butter. This is the purest form of chocolate.

To make the different kinds of chocolate, sugar, milk, and more cocoa butter are added.

UNSWEETENED CHOCOLATE

As the name implies, this chocolate has no sugar added. It is basically pure chocolate and is very bitter. Because it needs sugar, it is best used for baking and cooking such treats as cake and fudge.

CACAO OR COCOA?

Cacao is the purest form of chocolate. **Cocoa,** on the other hand, has gone through a very high heat process.

COCOA POWDER

Cocoa powder is ground up, unsweetened chocolate with most of the cocoa butter removed. Because it has a deep dark chocolate flavor, a little goes a long way. It is used to make candies, baked desserts, ice cream, and other foods. Add some sugar and hot milk and you have a very rich hot chocolate drink!

MILK CHOCOLATE

Milk chocolate is the sweetest and most popular of all chocolate products. Because milk has been added, it has a soft creamy texture that melts in your mouth. The added sugar makes it an ideal eating chocolate. It also can be used for baking or even to sweeten up pancakes and muffins.

DARK CHOCOLATE

The taste of this chocolate is more about the chocolate and less about the sugar. Some people think it is too bitter to be eaten. Other people prefer to eat it because of its low sugar content and intense chocolate flavor. It is also called *bittersweet* or *semisweet* chocolate, and it is used in cookies and cakes.

WHITE CHOCOLATE

The main ingredient in white chocolate is sweetened cocoa butter. It does not contain any cocoa solids—the stuff that gives chocolate its flavor and color. Because it is missing cocoa solids, some people think it is not real chocolate.

CHOCOLATE MAKES ITS WAY TO
ITALY

Chocolate made its introduction to Italy in the early 1600's as a beverage. The Italians experimented with different ways to make their chocolate drink. As a matter of fact, they were the first to mix chocolate with coffee. One such drink, called **bicerin,** was developed in the city of Turin. Bicerin (pronounced *bee chuh REEN)* is served hot in a clear glass so that the different layers of hot chocolate, **espresso** (strong black coffee), milk, and cream can be seen. Italian hot chocolate is thicker, more like pudding.

DID YOU KNOW that Nutella was created from a chocolate shortage? Cocoa was in short supply during World War II. This led Pietro Ferrero, a pastry maker from Piedmont, Italy, to add ground hazelnuts to his sweet chocolate spread to increase the quantity.

BACK IN TIME

Chocolate seems to take a step back in time in Modica, Sicily. The town still makes its most famous food the same way the ancient Aztec used to make it, by hand. Modica's unique dark chocolate is made from a grainy cocoa paste created by crushing roasted cocoa beans on a curved stone slab with a stone rolling pin.

Italians invented such dishes as chocolate dessert soup, chocolate custard, and chocolate **sorbet.** But they also began experimenting with chocolate by adding it as a flavor to many savory dishes, including soup, meat, and pasta.

Delicate little dumplings called gnocchi (pronounced *NYAWK kee*) are a popular pasta dish in Italy. This version pairs chocolate with butter and cheese to create a special treat. To make tender soft gnocchi, be careful not to overwork the dough and not to overcook them.

CHOCOLATE GNOCCHI
Serves 4

INGREDIENTS

One 15-oz. container ricotta cheese, preferably whole milk
2 eggs
2 tbsp. cocoa powder
1 ¼ cups freshly grated Parmesan cheese, plus more for serving

Salt
1 ¼ cups all-purpose flour, plus more for dusting
3 tsp. butter

STEPS

1. In a large bowl, mix the ricotta cheese, eggs, cocoa powder, Parmesan cheese, and a pinch of salt. Add in the flour in three equal parts, mixing well after each addition.
2. When all ingredients are combined, form the dough into a ball and divide it into four equal parts. If the dough is a bit tacky, coat your hands in flour to work with the dough.
3. Sprinkle flour on the work surface to prevent the dough from sticking. Using your hands, roll one section of dough into a long rope about ½ to ¾ inches in diameter. Don't worry if the dough isn't uniformly shaped!
4. Cut the rope into ¾-inch pieces. Using the back of a fork, gently roll one of the pieces of dough against the tines. Use just enough pressure to form shallow ridges. Place on a floured sheet pan, leaving space between them. Repeat until all the dough has been rolled, cut, and shaped.
5. Boil a large pot of water with a sprinkling of salt. Carefully add your gnocchi to the boiling water and cook for about 2-3 minutes, until they rise to the surface.
6. As the water begins to boil, melt butter in a large sauce pan over medium-low heat.
7. When the gnocchi have risen to the top of the water, remove them with a slotted spoon and place them in the saucepan with butter. Gently toss them until they are all coated with butter.

NOT JUST FOR DESSERT

Chocolate for dinner? Yes, Italian style! The word chocolate immediately brings to mind something sweet. But chocolate has been used in preparing appetizing dishes in some parts of the world for hundreds of years. It might be hard to imagine chicken or pasta covered with a delicious chocolate sauce, but in Italy such recipes date as far back as 1680. It became a common practice to season foods with chocolate, and the practice continues to this day. When used in cooking, however, chocolate should be added in small amounts so that the chocolate can not be tasted. It should help bring the flavors together in a dish, not be the star of dinner.

Many countries use chocolate to flavor a variety of dishes. Spain and South Africa add chocolate to such meat dishes as beef, game, or lobster. France and Mexico use it to make rich sauces, such as red wine sauce in France and mole (pronounced *moh lay*) in Mexico. Mole is popular for celebrations. It's served with chicken but goes great with enchiladas or beef. Mole is made with hot chili peppers and dark chocolate, which takes the heat out of the peppers.

GOOD STUFF!

Chocolate naturally contains about 300 different flavors and 400 different scents. Research shows that the smell of chocolate calms the nerves and promotes relaxation.

SAVORY TREATS!

Chocolate fried chicken is an American creation, along with chocolate ketchup, white chocolate mashed potatoes, and chocolate-seasoned fries.

SWITZERLAND

Chocolate made its transformation from a drink, or a flavor enhancer, into a smooth and creamy candy treat in the 1800's in Switzerland. This transformation was the genius of a few chocolate pioneers.

In 1819, François-Louis Cailler opened up a small chocolate factory in Corsey, near Vevey. Soon, the town of Vevey was a hub for chocolate production. Cailler also revolutionized the chocolate making process! Using a water-powered machine, Cailler made it possible to rapidly produce chocolate on a large scale. The faster chocolate could be made, the more popular it became.

In 1875, Cailler's son-in-law, Daniel Peter, invented milk chocolate! Peter began adding milk to chocolate as a way to reduce costs and make it taste better. His neighbor, Henri Nestlé, specialized in the condensed milk that Peter mixed with his chocolate liquid. Together, they had created milk chocolate!

DID YOU KNOW that Switzerland consumes more chocolate *per capita* (for each person) than any country in the world? The average Swiss eats about 20 pounds of chocolate a year. China, on the other hand, consumes the least amount of chocolate per capita, less than a half pound a year.

TRICKY COMBINATION

It is a well-known fact that water and oil do not mix. That explains why it is tricky to blend milk, a water-based product, with chocolate, an oil-based product. Water makes chocolate clump up.

MELTING POINT

Can you guess why chocolate melts in your mouth so easily? Chocolate melts at a temperature of around 93 °F (34 °C). That is just below the normal body temperature of human beings.

BELGIUM

Belgium's association with chocolate began in 1635, when Spain ruled the land. Today, Belgium is one of the top producers and exporters of chocolate. It is known worldwide for its creamy, delicious-tasting chocolates with such famous brands as Godiva and Neuhaus. A key to their success is an 1884 law requiring all products labeled "Belgian chocolate" to contain a minimum of 35 percent pure cocoa. Belgian chocolate makers pride themselves on making their chocolate with 100 percent cocoa butter.

BIGGEST CHOCOLATE SHOP!

Brussels Airport sells more chocolate than any place else in the world! Airport vendors sell over 800 tons of Belgium's finest chocolate brands each year. One of the vendors is the Belgian Chocolate House, which is the world's largest chocolate seller.

DID YOU KNOW that Belgium's world-famous praline chocolates were invented by a Swiss immigrant? In 1912, Jean Neuhaus II was the first to come up with a way to make hollow chocolate shells with a soft sweet filling. These deliciously addictive chocolates came to be known worldwide as **pralines.**

Brussels waffles are a traditional street food in Belgium. The proper way to eat them is plain and with your hands! Or just drizzle them with chocolate syrup.

PUTTING THE "MMMM" IN MAIL

Belgium once issued a limited edition of chocolate-flavored stamps!

AFRICA

West Africa has a climate similar to Central America, where cacao trees were first cultivated. West Africa's hot and rainy tropical climate provides ideal growing conditions for the delicate cacao plants. Cacao beans were brought to Africa by Christian missionaries in the early 1800's. Today, West Africa is the world's main source of chocolate. The African nations of Côte d'Ivoire, Ghana, Nigeria, and Cameroon produce and export more than 70 percent of all the cocoa in the world. Côte d'Ivoire, also known as the Ivory Coast, is the leading producer by far, with more than 33 percent of the world's supply.

DID YOU KNOW that in West Africa, cacao is grown almost entirely on small family farms? The average farm is about 7 to 10 acres in size. The whole family, along with friends and neighbors, help **harvest** the cacao crop. All of the work is done by hand!

SWEAT IT OUT!

The rich chocolate flavor and aroma that we know and love comes from fermenting the cocoa beans. This involves covering the bitter-tasting beans with banana leaves for a few days.

A WORLD WITHOUT CHOCOLATE?

Some scientists predict there could be a major shortage of chocolate in the future! The problem is that we are eating more chocolate than we can produce. Demand is increasing worldwide. Cacao farmers are producing less and can't keep up with demand. Every year, they lose 30 percent of their crop to disease and global weather problems, such as rising temperatures and *drought* (a long time without rain).

Cacao farmers in West Africa produce over three-fourths of all the world's cocoa. But the farmers reap little benefit from their hard labor in this profitable global trade. Most live in poverty and struggle to survive. Most have never even tasted chocolate! It's too expensive for them to eat. In fact, chocolate consumption in all of Africa accounts for only about 3 percent of the world's supply.

TAKING SHAPE

The machine age brought about great improvements to the taste and texture of chocolate. Machines also made it easier and quicker to produce chocolate in large amounts and at a lower cost. This made chocolate available to everyone, not just the rich and famous.

Dutch chemist Coenraad Van Houten invented the cocoa press in 1829. He was able to turn chocolate into a powder by squeezing all the cocoa butter out of the bean. Today we call this cocoa powder or just cocoa. Van Houten also created a way to help cocoa mix better with water. He added alkaline salts to cocoa to cut the bitter taste. This process, called "dutching," gives chocolate its dark color and mild taste. As a result of Van Houten's inventions, chocolate had a better taste and a smooth and creamy texture.

Van Houten's cocoa press enabled chocolatiers to make a variety of chocolate flavors just by mixing together different amounts of cocoa powder and cocoa butter. The cocoa press paved the way for making such delicious treats as white chocolate, milk chocolate, and hot chocolate, as well as for using cocoa in baking.

A LONG TIME!

Chocolate was consumed as a liquid, not a solid, for 90 percent of its history.

DID YOU KNOW that the Hershey Chocolate Company makes 70 million chocolate kisses a day? That's enough to stretch 300,000 miles long if you put them all in a row. The Hershey company was founded in 1894 by American manufacturer Milton S. Hershey in Derry Church (now Hershey), Pennsylvania.

THE CHOCOLATE BAR

The world's first chocolate bar was made in the United Kingdom by J. S. Fry & Sons in 1847. The company made a paste of cocoa powder and sugar and molded it into a bar shape. This was the first popular form of eating chocolate. The chocolate bar was further developed by John Cadbury, who introduced his famous brand in 1849.

Other companies, such as Hershey, Nestlé, Tobler, Cadbury, and Guylian, began making their own chocolate bars. In the early 1900's, they introduced over 200 new products, including the first wrapped chocolate bar, chocolate truffles, **pralines,** and the first chocolate Easter egg.

WORLD RECORD!

The world's largest chocolate bar weighed more than 12,770 pounds (5,792.50 kilograms)! It was made by Thorntons candy company and set a Guinness World Record. It was later broken up into pieces and sold to raise money for charity.

Snickers is the world's best-selling chocolate candy bar. More than 15 million Snickers are produced each day. It is one of the three main types of chocolate bars: solid milk chocolate, solid dark chocolate, and chocolate with fillings. Such candy fillings include nuts, caramel, fruit, and nougat.

BEYOND THE BAR

As the taste and texture of chocolate became more refined, the possibilities for its use greatly increased. Today, the sweet taste of chocolate can be added to just about anything. It can be whipped into frosting or baked into a cupcake or even hardened as a covering over pretzels. What would an ice cream sundae be without a velvety smooth hot fudge sauce?

DID YOU KNOW that the term s'*more* is a shortened form of the words "some more"? The tasty treat made of graham crackers, a toasted marshmallow, and a chocolate bar was supposedly invented in 1925 by a Girl Scout troop! The Hershey Company makes enough chocolate bars a year to produce over 740 million s'mores.

MISTAKEN IDENTITY!

German chocolate cake did not come from Germany. It was invented by an American baker named Sam German.

Chocolate brownies are one of the most popular baked goods in the United States. No one knows exactly how brownies got their start. One story is that a baker forgot to add a rising agent to the chocolate cake batter. When the cake came out of the oven it was flat. The baker served it anyway, and a fudgy cake was born!

TRY THIS!

CHOCOLATE BROWNIES

Makes 16 squares

INGREDIENTS

½ cup cocoa powder
1 cup flour
½ cup salted butter, melted
½ cup room temperature coffee

1 tsp. vanilla extract
1 ¼ cup sugar
3 eggs

STEPS

1. Preheat the oven to 350 °F (175 °C). Line an 8-inch x 8-inch baking pan with aluminum foil; make sure foil overlaps sides.
2. Mix cocoa and flour in a bowl.
3. In a large bowl, stir together melted butter, coffee, vanilla, and sugar. Whisk in eggs for about a minute. All the whisking will result in a crackly top. Slowly stir the flour and cocoa into the butter mixture just until combined. Over mixing at this stage will create air pockets, resulting in cakelike brownies. Pour batter into the lined baking pan and smooth out the top.
4. Bake at 350 °F (175 °C) for 30 to 35 minutes, or until a toothpick inserted in the center comes out clean for more cakelike brownies. For fudgy brownies, a toothpick will come out with just a little chocolate on it. Remove brownies from the oven and let them cool to room temperature. Then, lift the brownies out of the pan and cut them into 4 rows of 4.

HOLIDAYS

Valentine's Day, Easter, Halloween, Christmas, Hanukkah, Diwali in India, Day of the Dead in Mexico, and many other holidays are celebrated throughout the world with chocolate.

Chocolate Easter eggs made their first appearance in France and Germany in the early 1800's, followed by the chocolate bunny. This tradition has spread across the globe. In Australia, eating chocolate Easter eggs is considered to be the country's biggest chocolate eating holiday.

NO FOOLING!

In France, fish-shaped chocolate is given out for April Fool's Day, which is called. "Poisson d'Avril". The French word *poisson* translates to fish.

Throughout history, chocolate was given as gifts or served at weddings. It is no wonder that today, chocolate is still considered the perfect gift for Valentine's Day. The tradition started in 1861 when the English chocolate company Cadbury packaged the sweets into heart-shaped boxes. In Japan and Korea, however, it is the guy who expects to receive the chocolate gift from the girl!

DID YOU KNOW

that more than twice as much chocolate is sold for Halloween as it is for Valentine's Day?

WHAT A DAY!

September 13th is International Chocolate Day.

NOT FOR EVERYONE

Although it is fun to receive and eat chocolate, it should never be given to your pets. Chocolate can make an animal very sick.

Chocolate coins wrapped in gold foil are given as little treats during the Jewish Hanukkah holiday.

ENERGY BOOST

Just a small piece of chocolate is enough to give you an energy boost. That's why throughout history chocolate has traveled with explorers. Americans Meriwether Lewis and William Clark drank chocolate on their historic expedition across the northwestern United States. So did Norwegian explorer Roald Amundsen on his journey to the South Pole. Eating chocolate kept American aviator Amelia Earhart going on her solo flight across the Atlantic in 1932. Soldiers, past and present, have been given chocolate as part of their military food rations. Astronauts snack on chocolates, too, to keep up their energy levels while in space.

It is the nutrients in chocolate that help keep you physically going. That's why some athletes drink chocolate milk after exercising. The darker the chocolate, the more nutrients! But you don't need a lot. A little more than half the average candy bar will do the trick!

ON THE GO!

Napoleon Bonaparte, the French military and political leader, used chocolate as a quick energy snack. He took it with him on military campaigns.

A LITTLE GOES A LONG WAY!

One chocolate chip can give a person enough energy to walk 150 feet.

STARRING ROLE

Who wouldn't want to ride on a river of chocolate! Such adventures can be read about in a book or watched on a movie screen.

Roald Dahl's 1964 children's book, *Charlie and the Chocolate Factory,* became a modern classic. The fantasy novel is about a poor boy named Charlie and four other children who win a tour of the magical Wonka Chocolate Factory and a chance to win a lifetime supply of chocolate! Dahl's book was adapted into two motion pictures and a musical production.

REALLY WONKA

Fiction became reality with the launch of a real-life Willy Wonka Candy Company in 1971. Wonka Candy sold real Wonka bars based on the fictional candies in Dahl's book. Wonka bars are still sold today.

DID YOU KNOW that the chocolate river in the 1971 movie *Willy Wonka & the Chocolate Factory* was real? It was made of 150,000 gallons of water mixed with real chocolate and cream.

SWEET MAGIC!

Chocolate frog candy became a reality with the success of the Harry Potter books and movies.

Chocolate is the star of the show at the world's first chocolate theme park in Beijing, China. World Chocolate Wonderland allows visitors to "see, touch, taste, and smell" chocolate. There you can see a giant chocolate fountain and lifelike chocolate miniatures of the Great Wall of China, the Forbidden City, and the famous terra-cotta warriors.

GLOSSARY

bicerin *(bee chuh REEN)* A famous warm chocolate and coffee drink from Turin, Italy.

cacao *(kuh KAY oh)* The seeds from which cocoa and chocolate are made.

chocolatier *(CHAWK luh tihr)* A person who creates recipes and decorative desserts made from chocolate.

cocoa *(koh koh)* A brown powder made from roasting and grinding cocoa beans and that is used to make chocolate.

colonial *(kuh LOH nee uhl)* Of or having to do with a colony; the 13 British colonies that became the United States of America.

conche *(konsh)* A machine for processing chocolate into a fine texture.

counterfeit *(KOUN tuhr fit)* Not real; to fake; copy.

espresso *(ehs PREHS oh)* A very strong black coffee made of coffee beans roasted black, and brewed under steam pressure, usually in a special machine.

ferment *(fuhr MEHNT)* A biological process carried out by microbes, such as bacteria, molds, and yeasts, that breaks down materials.

harvest To gather a crop; the act of gathering a crop.

indigenous *(ihn DIHJ uh nuhs)* Native to a region.

ingredient *(ihn GREE dee uhnt)* A thing that is mixed with others; one of the parts of a mixture.

molinillo *(moh lee NEE yoh)* A special wooden whisk that is rolled back and forth between the palms to create foam in hot beverages.

nibs The roasted and crushed seeds of the cacao; cocoa nibs.

nobility *(noh BIHL uh tee)* People of high rank, usually with great wealth and power.

pralines *(PRAH leen)* Chocolates with flavored fillings.

profiterole *(pruh FIHT uh ROHL)* A small, light puff of pastry, with such filling as ice cream, whipped cream, fruit, or creamed meat or fish.

sorbet *(sawr BAY)* A dessert ice made of fruit or juice. It has a smooth, creamy texture.

HELPFUL HINTS

When working in the kitchen with food, keep these helpful hints in mind to make sure your work goes smoothly and safely. Then enjoy the tasty treats you make!

- **Wash your hands** before you begin food preparation and after you've touched raw eggs or meat.
- Thoroughly **wash fruits and vegetables.**
- **Use oven mitts** when handling hot pots, pans, or trays.
- **Have an adult help** when working with knives and hot stoves or ovens.

INDEX

World Book, Inc.
180 North LaSalle Street
Suite 900
Chicago, Illinois 60601
USA

For information about other "Taste the World!" titles, as well as other World Book print and digital publications, please go to www.worldbook.com.

For information about other World Book publications, call 1-800-WORLDBK (967-5325).

For information about sales to schools and libraries, call 1-800-975-3250 (United States) or 1-800-837-5365 (Canada).

Library of Congress Cataloging-in-Publication Data

Title: Chocolate.
Description: Chicago, Illinois: World Book Inc., 2020. | Series: Taste the world! | Includes index.
Identifiers: LCCN 2019037152 | ISBN 9780716628590 (hardcover) | ISBN 9780716628583 (set)
Subjects: LCSH: Cooking (Chocolate)--History--Juvenile literature. | Chocolate--History--Juvenile literature.
Classification: LCC TX767.C5 C537 2020 | DDC 641.6/374--dc23
LC record available at https://lccn.loc.gov/2019037152

Taste the World!
ISBN: 978-0-7166-2858-3 (set, hc.)

Chocolate
ISBN: 978-0-7166-2859-0 (hc.)

Also available as:
ISBN: 978-0-7166-2867-5 (e-book)

2nd printing July 2020

STAFF

Editorial

Writer: Mellonee Carrigan

Manager, New Product Development
Nick Kilzer

Proofreader: Nathalie Strassheim

Manager, Contracts and Compliance
(Rights and Permissions): Loranne K. Shields

Manager, Indexing Services
David Pofelski

Digital

Director, Digital Product Development
Erika Meller

Digital Product Manager
Jonathan Wills

Graphics and Design

Coordinator, Design Development
and Production
Brenda Tropinski

Senior Visual Communications Designer
Melanie Bender

Media Editor: Rosalia Bledsoe

Senior Web Designer/Digital Media Developer
Matt Carrington

Manufacturing/Production

Manufacturing Manager: Anne Fritzinger

Production Specialist: Curley Hunter

ACKNOWLEDGMENTS

Cover   © Art Nick/Shutterstock; © Jiri Hera, Shutterstock; © Sherlesi/Shutterstock
Character artwork by Matthew Carrington
2-3   © Shutterstock; Public Domain (Codex Tudela); NASA/JSC
4-7   © Shutterstock
8-9   © Diego Grandi, Shutterstock; © Justin Kerr, Maya Vase Database; *Tripod Vessel with Supernatural Palace Scene and Cacao Tree* (Guatemala, Peten, Motul de San José or vicinity, Maya, 750-850), slip-painted ceramic; Los Angeles County Museum of Art
10-11   © Jiri Hera, Shutterstock; © National Geographic Image Collection/Alamy Images; © Roger Viollet Collection/Getty Images
12-13   Public Domain (Codex Tudela); © AGCuesta/Shutterstock; © Ray Waddington, Alamy Images; © Marcos Castillo, Shutterstock
14-15   © Ridkous Mykhailo, Shutterstock; © Album/Alamy Images; © Bartosz Luczak, Shutterstock; Public Domain (New York Public Library)
16-17   *The family of the Duke of Penthièvre called la tasse de chocolat* (1768), oil on canvas by Jean-Baptiste Charpentier; Palace of Versailles (Leemage/Corbis/Getty Images); © Sherlesi/Shutterstock; Public Domain; © Africa Studio/Shutterstock
18-19   © Sylvain Lefevre, Getty Images; © Westend61/Getty Images; © Sylvain Lefevre, Getty Images; © Patrick Kovarik, Getty Images; © Jiri Hera, Shutterstock
20-23   © Shutterstock
24-25   © Moreno Novello, Dreamstime; © Gresei/Shutterstock; WORLD BOOK photos by Rosalia Bledsoe
26-29   © Shutterstock
30-31   © Grezova Olga, Shutterstock; © Manfred Segerer, ullstein bild/Getty Images
32-33   © GianLuigi Guercia, Getty Images; © Wicki58/iStockphoto
34-35   © Rafael Ben Ari, Dreamstime; © Igors Rusakovs, Shutterstock; © Skodonnell/iStockphoto
36-37   © Mars, Incorporated; © Shutterstock
38-39   © Art Nick/Shutterstock; © Brenda Carson, Shutterstock; WORLD BOOK photo by Brenda Tropinski
40-41   © Wendy Maeda, The Boston Globe/Getty Images; © Tiger Images/Shutterstock; © Photastic/Shutterstock; © Leena Robinson, Shutterstock; © Tomertu/Shutterstock
42-43   NASA/JSC; © Baibaz/Shutterstock; © David E. Scherman, The LIFE Picture Collection/Getty Images; © Everett Historical/Shutterstock; Library of Congress; National Library of Norway
44-45   © Stephen Clarke, Shutterstock; © Paramount Pictures; © Warner Bros.; © STR/AFP/Getty Images

www.ingramcontent.com/pod-product-compliance
Lightning Source LLC
Chambersburg PA
CBHW041047050726
47599CB00018B/2076